Alternative Programs

for Students with Social, Emotional or Behavioral Problems

Mary Magee Quinn
Center for Effective Collaboration and Practice
American Institutes for Research

Robert B. Rutherford, Jr.
Arizona State University

Lyndal M. Bullock & Robert A. Gable, *Series Editors*

The Council for Children with Behavioral Disorders, *Publisher*

About the Council for Children with Behavioral Disorders

CCBD is an international professional organization committed to promoting and facilitating the education and general welfare of children and youth with behavioral and emotional disorders. CCBD, whose members include educators, parents, mental health personnel, and a variety of other professionals, actively pursues quality educational services and program alternatives for persons with behavioral disorders, advocates for the needs of such children and youth, emphasizes research and professional growth as vehicles for better understanding behavioral disorders, and provides professional support for persons who are involved with and serve children and youth with behavioral disorders.

In advocating for the professionals in the field of behavioral disorders, CCBD (a division of The Council for Exceptional Children) endorses the Standards for Professional Practice and Code of Ethics adopted by the Delegate Assembly of The Council for Exceptional Children in 1983.

About This Monograph

Stock No. D5238, ISBN 0-86586-304-0

Printed in the United States of America

10   9   8   7   6   5   4   3   2

Contents

Foreword

This is the second mini-library series that addresses the needs of students identified as "seriously emotionally disturbed" or "emotionally/behaviorally disordered." As with the first series, the content stems from selected presentations at an international conference sponsored by the Council for Children with Behavioral Disorders (CCBD). These monographs are also a response to the reality that the number of children and youth who evidence challenging behavior is growing. These students manifest a range of social, academic, and behavior problems that test the skills of even the most capable classroom teachers. Educators and other professionals are struggling to find ways to deal successfully with the mounting challenges these students present.

Fortunately, as the number of problems increases, so too does the body of accumulated literature on practices of proven effectiveness for students with emotional/behavioral disorders (EBD). Drawing upon the expertise of CCBD members, we have assembled a seven-volume series of monographs that delve into some of the specific areas and programs for students with EBD and the education professionals who work with them:

- *Alternative Programs for Students with Social, Emotional, or Behavioral Problems*
  Mary Magee Quinn and Robert B. Rutherford, Jr.

- *Curriculum and Instruction Practices for Students with Emotional / Behavioral Disorders*
  Rex E. Schmid and William Evans, Editors

- *Developing Personal and Interpersonal Responsibility in Children and Youth with Emotional/Behavioral Disorders*
  Sylvia Rockwell, Santa Cuccio, Beth Kirtley, and Gwen Smith

- *Developing Social Competence in Children and Youth with Challenging Behaviors*
  Kristine J. Melloy, Carol A. Davis, Joseph H. Wehby, Francie R. Murry, and Jennifer Leiber

- *Enhancing Self-Respect: A Challenge for Teachers of Students with Emotional/Behavioral Disorders*
  Ann Fitzsimons-Lovett

- *Individual and Systemic Approaches to Collaboration and Consultation on Behalf of Students with Emotional/Behavioral Disorders*
  Robert A. Gable, George Sugai, Tim Lewis, J. Ron Nelson, Douglas Cheney, Stephen P. Safran, and Joan S. Safran

- *Teaching Children and Youth Self-Control: Applications of Perceptual Control Theory*
  John W. Maag

In these seven monographs, we have attempted to bring together information that addresses the needs of general and special educators, administrators, and other professionals who face the myriad challenges of children and youth at risk for or with EBD. We are grateful for the contributions of the monograph authors and hopeful that their efforts will prove useful to you in your work on behalf of students with EBD.

Lyndal M. Bullock
University of North Texas

Robert A. Gable
Old Dominion University

Series Editors

Introduction 1

There is little consensus regarding what constitutes an appropriate *alternative placement* for children and youth with social, emotional, and behavioral problems. Programs identified as "alternatives" range from short-term, in-school suspension rooms (housed within a regular school program) to separate residential facilities designed for intensive, long-term care and treatment. Each of these kinds of programs, technically speaking, represents "alternative approaches to regular education" and can be accounted for by changing educational philosophy and the associated issues that arise from such changes.

Because the purpose of this monograph is to examine educational alternatives for children and youth with emotional, behavioral, or social problems, we will focus on the just enumerated alternatives to traditional education systems, concentrating on those which have an administrative structure separate from the regular education system. We begin with a brief description of the role alternative programs have played during the last few decades and their varying roles within the continuum of placements today. We then examine the major issues that dictate practices in alternative programs nationwide. Components of effective alternative programs will be highlighted and suggestions provided for changes to improve the current practices in some alternative programs.

We also examine the paradox resulting from attempts at the full inclusion of students with disabilities and the special difficulties that traditional education systems face when disciplining students with

emotional, behavioral, or social disorders who are included in mainstream education placements. Finally, we attempt to deal with the
controversial question, "Is it the system or the student who needs to
change?"

From Stopgap to Prevention: Alternative School Models

2

Alternative programs first gained popularity in the 1950s and 1960s, at which time they were designed to educate people who had already dropped out of school. Today, the focus of most alternative programs is preventive in nature; they provide students at risk of dropping out with an individualized system of supports not usually available in traditional educational settings (Glass, 1994). While most alternative programs are currently designed for high-school-aged youth, there appears to be a trend toward providing alternative programs to middle school students who need the social, behavioral, emotional, and academic support necessary to prevent them from dropping out.

Aware that many students become disillusioned with the traditional educational system and, therefore, do drop out (or, in some cases, that the traditional educational system becomes disillusioned with students and expels or suspends them), those who develop alternative programs seek to provide an appropriate education for students who might otherwise never receive a high school diploma. Alternative programs provide students with "some place to go other than the streets and more trouble when they're expelled from regular school" (Glass, 1994, p. 10). The most effective alternative programs accomplish this self-determined mission by providing education not only in an alternative setting but also in an alternative manner, with most including flexible curricula molded to address the individual student's social, behavioral, emotional, cognitive, and vocational needs. This one-to-one correspondence between student need and curricular content is touted as one of the main reasons that some alternative programs are more successful than others.

While there are no globally accepted assessment tools to measure this kind of effectiveness, there are, nevertheless, several indicators that can be used to gauge success (Ball, 1997). For example, successful outcomes are indicated by significant increases in attendance, by an increase in achievement, by increased graduation rates, by parent involvement, and by the reduction of discipline referrals. Changes in attitude and behavior, reflected in these outcomes, serve to pave the way for students to return to their home-schools or to enter the work force. The programs have, in effect, given their students a better chance at becoming productive citizens.

Generally, at-risk students are placed in alternative school programs once it is determined that chronic disruptive and norm-violating behaviors will prohibit them from attaining academic and social success in regular school environments (Fuller & Sabatino, 1996). As previously noted, a variety of alternative school programs have been developed to serve this ever-increasing population of youth who have left or been elbowed out of traditional public schools. Examples include school-within-a-school programs, alternative schools, continuation schools, court schools, detention schools, probation camp schools, and charter schools. The vignette comprising Appendix A is an example of one effective alternative to traditional education programs.

School-within-a-School Programs

Programs known as schools-within-a-school are housed within a traditional school but offer "autonomous" or "specialized" programs apart from the mainstream. Such programs generally operate in a wing or cluster of "portables" on the main school campus, separate from the larger student body. While such programs often are independently administered, the goal of most school-within-a-school programs is to eventually return students to the traditional school program.

Alternative Schools

By far the most prevalent model of alternative programming, separate schools are operated by the public schools as an option for students who have failed to "make it" in traditional schools. These alternative schools usually are designed as punitive environments wherein students expelled from a traditional education setting receive some type of "treatment" that is supposed to teach them the skills necessary for their return to mainstream programs.

Continuation Schools

Continuation programs are designed for students who no longer attend traditional schools but who wish to continue their education. These "second chance" schools include "street academics" or other, job-related training centers, and "parenting centers" for teenage mothers who want to graduate from high school (Smink, 1997). Continuation schools are what Raywid (1994) describes as Innovative or Type I schools, wherein students voluntarily attend because they value the curriculum.

Court Schools, Detention Schools, Probation Camp Schools

A number of alternative school programs are operated by the juvenile justice system, rather than by the public school system. These so-called Type II programs (Raywid, 1994) are designed for youth who, because of criminal behavior, are committed by the courts to restrictive programs. While court schools are usually community-based day programs for offenders, detention centers and probation camps are custodial facilities in which education is offered in conjunction with incarceration. These correctional programs are often of short duration, and students either return to other community-based alternative programs or to traditional school programs — or, sadly, become submerged deeper and deeper into the corrections system, often ending in state juvenile reformatories or adult correctional programs.

Charter Schools

A relatively recent phenomenon involves the development of private "charter" schools. Charter schools are tax-supported alternative programs usually located off traditional school campuses in community-based settings. These schools are small, with fewer than 100 students, and autonomous in the sense that they do not have to follow many of the rules and regulations imposed on public school programs. About half of them are intended to serve primarily at-risk students (Smink, 1997).

Issues in Alternative Education

3

To Include or Not to Include

Many students educated in alternative settings have been identified as having a disability of some kind. In fact, the specific issue of alternative programs for students with emotional/behavioral disorders (EBD) was recently spotlighted as a result of the debate in the educational community over *where* the education of students with exceptional needs should take place. In response to this concern, the authors of Public Law 94-142, and its later reauthorization, the Individuals with Disabilities Education Act (IDEA), had included in official legislation that children with disabilities should be educated in the "least restrictive environment" (LRE). The IDEA, for instance, specifically states that

> to the maximum extent appropriate, children with disabilities, including children in public or private institutions or other care facilities, [must be] educated with children who are non-disabled. (34 CFR 300.550 (b) 1)

Significantly, this one phrase has produced more debate than perhaps any other single component of the IDEA legislation.

The concept of a LRE has evolved and been adjusted over the past two decades to reflect changes in the belief systems and attitudes of the educational community. The term has been interpreted by some to simply mean the least restrictive "physical setting" in which a child receives educational services. In contrast, proponents of *full inclusion* equate LRE exclusively with a general education classroom. To others, LRE means that the continuum of placements provided for in the original federal legislation should be considered to determine which setting within the system of service delivery provides the least restrictive setting in which to meet the needs of individual students. On this point, the IDEA states that

> a continuum of alternative placements is available to meet the needs of children with disabilities for special education and related services (34CFR 300.551 (a)) and provide supplementary services (such as resource rooms or aides) to be provided in conjunction with regular class placement. (34 CFR 300.551(b))

The various interpretations of LRE have led to widespread, often contentious debates embroiling many caring professionals involved in serving children and youth with disabilities. The controversy has recently escalated due to discussions about the "appropriateness" of full inclusion into the general education classroom. Proponents of full inclusion feel that all students with disabilities should be placed in age-appropriate, regular classes for the entire school day. Critics of that interpretation of inclusion argue that "no single placement is universally beneficial to all students with disabilities" (MacMillan, Gresham, & Forness, 1996, p. 150).

Adding fuel to the debate, many professional organizations dedicated to the education of children and youth with disabilities have taken positions regarding the issue of full inclusion. For example, the Council of Administrators of Special Education (1994), the Council for Exceptional Children (1993), and the National Association of State Boards of Education (1992) have developed position papers regarding the delivery of services to students with disabilities. According to the Council of Administrators of Special Education, "inclusion means that students with disabilities are educated in supported, heterogeneous, age-appropriate, and natural and student-centered classroom, school, and community environments for the purpose of preparing them for full participation in a diverse and integrated society" (p. 2). It is the position of these organizations, however, that inclusion is *more than just a physical location* and that decisions regarding the educational placement of students with disabilities should be made on an individual basis, using the full continuum of placement options.

Although the philosophy and practice of full physical inclusion is being attempted in many school districts across the nation, the practice remains particularly difficult to apply when trying to adequately address the immensely diverse needs of children with EBD (MacMillan et al., 1996). Actually, many parents and professionals believe that, in terms of full inclusion for all children *with disabilities*, the term "all" does not include those children with emotional or behavioral problems. Many parents and professionals contend that it is "not in the best interest" of the child with the disability to educate potentially violent or otherwise persistently disruptive students in mainstream settings.

At this point, it should be made clear that the needs of the students are not the only concern in the full inclusion debate. Professional teacher unions such as the American Federation of Teachers have stated that they also are concerned with the effects of full inclusion on general education teachers, arguing that most teachers have not been trained to handle nor do they have a support system that can sufficiently meet the variety of needs of students with emotional or behavioral problems (American Federation of Teachers, 1993, p. 264).

Within the Paradox: Discipline

A staggering number of school districts across the nation are plagued with discipline problems and have developed firm consequences for students whose behavior threatens the safety of themselves, their classmates, or adults who work in schools. Many districts responding to the public outcry to expel, without question, any student who infringes upon school safety have adopted a policy of "zero tolerance" for students who possess weapons or illegal drugs while on school property.

Suspension and expulsion have, of course, long been the punishments of choice for students who display either unsafe, violent, or persistently disruptive behaviors. However, current legislation limits the total number of days that a student with disabilities can be suspended, and then only after it has been determined that "the misconduct is not related to the student's disability" (Egnor, 1996, p. 18). Further, these "regular" disciplinary procedures can be imposed only "subject to the parents' right to request a due process hearing on whether the manifestation determination was correct" (p. 18). Although the IDEA does not specifically address the issue of discipline of students with disabilities, it does contain what has been termed the "stay-put" provision. This provision limits to 45 days the local education agency's power to change a student's placement. If the local education agency desires to change the child's placement beyond the 45 days, the child's parents have the right to appeal during which the child is returned to his or her initial placement (previous to the interim alternative placement) (P.L. 105-17, Part b, Sec. 615(k)(7)(B).

What this modification to the rule means is that the philosophies of full inclusion and zero tolerance are contradictory and, therefore, place administrators of traditional educational institutions in a paradoxical predicament. Students with disabilities are to be "fully included" in the general education program, but they cannot *by law* be disciplined in traditional ways.

Many professionals have reacted to this paradox by advocating changes to the current legislation. Professional teachers' unions, such as the American Federation of Teachers and the National Education Association, in concert with several other professional organizations (e.g., National School Boards Association, National Association of Elementary School Principals, National Association of Secondary School Principals) have proposed changes that would mandate the removal of all students who are violent or persistently disruptive from the general education setting and move them into alternative placements (Egnor, 1996).

The Council for Children with Behavioral Disorders (CCBD) and the Council of Administrators of Special Education (CASE; 1995)

Alternative Programs for Students

have addressed the issue of discipline of students with disabilities whose behavior is violent or otherwise aggressive. They have underscored the point that most acts of aggression and violence in schools are not perpetrated by children identified as having EBD. In fact, both organizations conclude that most incidences of violence are generated by nondisabled students who, due to a particular emotional crisis, react with inappropriate behavior.

Nonetheless, these two professional organizations endorse the immediate removal of any student with a disability from school whose behavior is "violent, aggressive, or destructive." They also suggest that these students should continue to receive an appropriate education in an alternative setting, until the time that an assessment has been completed and appropriate decisions regarding long-term educational placements can be made. This view is in accordance with the 1988 Supreme Court decision *Honig v. Doe*, in which the Court stated that a student with disabilities can be removed only with the permission of his or her parents or the courts.

Broken Children or Broken Systems?

Professionals charged with the care of students with EBD have long been unable to specifically identify the reason why some children and youth fail to thrive in traditional classroom settings. Some believe that the problem lies within the student, and that it is the student who is "different" or "broken." Others argue that the traditional system of education is, in fact, broken and, in its stagnancy, has become ineffective in meeting the diverse and rapidly changing needs of young people in today's society (Fizzell & Raywid, 1997). As always, such a double view does little to clarify "what to do next."

According to the literature examining the characteristics of students in alternative programs, many students share several common traits and often can be described as "cynical, suffering academic and behavioral adjustment problems in school, possessing antisocial attitudes and behaviors, lacking educational and/or career goals, and having problematic relationships with both family and peers" (Fuller & Sabatino, 1996, p. 295). While this may indicate to some that these children deviate from the norm, or are "broken," it does not explain the cause of that damage.

On the other hand are those who believe, as did the late Nick Hobbs, that emotional disturbance is a symptom not of individual pathology but of a malfunctioning ecosystem. Followers of Hobbs's philosophy advocate that adults have a responsibility to change that system in order to facilitate the child's growth in competence, freedom, responsibility, and self-respect. Therefore, when a child fails to learn and grow, the fault lies with the system and the adults responsible for the system (Hobbs, 1975).

For those who "blame the system," effective, nontraditional systems of education also share common philosophical tenets that deviate markedly from more traditional norms. Three beliefs have been identified by Raywid (1994) as underlying those alternative programs that are most effective. These beliefs are

1. A school, its students, and staff should function much the same as a community, with a great deal of effort spent developing a "strong sense of connection among students, and between students and teachers" (p. 29).

2. Learning should not only meet the individual needs of students but also be conducted in a way that fully engages all students. In sum, learning should be relevant and interesting and should compel the student to *want* to know more.

3. Schools must provide the structure and organization to make the first two elements "happen" in a consistent manner.

It is unclear whether a learning environment of this nature should, in fact, be an exception or a norm. Indeed, effective alternative educational systems with similar philosophical foundations would seem to be establishments with whom parents, students ("broken" or not), and educators would quite simply desire to be affiliated.

Clearly, however, there are discernible characteristics that segregate students who are educated in alternative settings from those who prosper in more traditional settings; and, conversely, there are identifiable components of nontraditional systems that effectively educate students who have diverse needs. To children in trouble and their families, these arguments are little more than academic. Perhaps a more practical question would be: *What are the components of systems that effectively meet the diverse, ever changing needs of children for whom the traditional setting does not work?* This question should lead to an examination of the role that any educational institution should or might play. That role could be further delineated by examining the curriculum and the type of services that students receive.

Types of Alternative Schools

4

Alternative programs can be described by what Raywid (1994) calls the three possible types of alternative schools:

1. *Innovative Schools,* which can be classified as *Type I,* were developed as an alternative to traditional schools by establishing organizational and administrative structures, as well as programmatic innovations, that are intentionally different from traditional educational structures and programs. These schools, from the point of view of their advocates, are designed to make schooling more humane, challenging, and compelling to students.

2. *Type II, or Last Chance Schools,* are punitive programs to which students are assigned or sentenced — usually representing "one last chance" prior to expulsion or placement in even more restrictive programs. Last Chance programs are designed for students who have failed to meet behavior or achievement norms and thus have been placed in highly structured, closely regulated programs that employ firm and aggressive disciplinary policies that have little to do with student options or choices.

3. *Remedial Schools (Type III)* are designed for students who are presumed to need academic and/or social and emotional remediation or rehabilitation. The assumption within remedial programs is that students, once "treated," can return to main-

stream programs. Remedial schools provide intensive counseling, extraordinary support, and intensive remediation to stimulate student's social, emotional, and academic growth. Placement in Type III alternative programs is generally by referral.

The premise upon which Innovative Schools are based assumes that traditional public schools have failed many students and that, by modifying the way schooling is delivered, those same students can and will survive and thrive. Both Last Chance and Remedial Schools seek to "fix" the student who is "broken," on the assumption that most "problems" lie within the individual. Innovative Schools, then, adapt education to meet the needs of individual students, while Last Chance and Remedial Schools view traditional programming as adequate for those students who are willing to fit in and actually be students. These latter schools are designed to change attitudes and behaviors and to provide students with the skills necessary for success in traditional classrooms.

Innovative Schools typically offer a curriculum believed by proponents to be superior to the traditional public school curriculum. In contrast, Last Chance Schools generally attempt to offer a traditional school curriculum, and Remedial Schools often limit the curriculum to very basic academics, with emphasis placed upon developing "functional skills" leading to "transition" into the world of work.

Educational or Custodial?

Alternative schools often differ from one another with regard to whether they are performing educational or custodial roles in terms of how students are assigned to programs. Innovative Schools focus on providing quality educational options that are appealing and individually tailored for students so that students *want* to come to school. Last Chance Schools focus, in fact, on mandatory placement for students who have been expelled form traditional classrooms. Remedial Schools, though, attempt to balance these views by focusing upon providing a quality education and by ensuring that students stay in school.

Alternative programs also vary in terms of services and of the ways those services are provided. Some alternative schools are strictly designed to deliver educational services. Other programs view themselves as social service agencies, offering extensive social and emotional as well as educational support. Still other alternative programs provide basic support while establishing links to other social service agencies.

Components of Effective Alternative Schools 5

Alternative schools offer opportunities as well as problems for education in general and special education in particular. There are six essential components of effective education, and those components, which are critical to the implementation of meaningful educational programs for disabled and nondisabled students, are frequently missing in many alternative programs (Rutherford & Howell, 1997; Rutherford, Nelson, & Wolford, 1985). They include

- Procedures for conducting functional assessments of the skills and learning needs of the student.

- A flexible curriculum that teaches functional academic, social, and daily living skills.

- Effective and efficient instructional techniques.

- Transitional programs and procedures that tie the alternative school to the public schools and to the community.

- Comprehensive systems for providing both internal alternative school services and external community services to students.

- Availability of appropriate staff and resources for students with disabilities.

Ineffective practices that exist in many alternative settings relative to these components are described next along with recommended practices for strengthening program components.

Functional Assessment of Student's Skills

Functional assessment is a set of practices designed to identify skill deficits that interfere with a student's educational achievement and social and emotional adjustment. This approach to assessment directly corresponds with the curriculum taught in the classes rather than being focused on global achievement or ability measures. Assessment should be continuous, rather than static, and results should be used to make systematic adjustments in the student's educational program (Howell, Fox, & Morehead, 1993).

Typical Practices in Many Alternative Programs

Assessment in alternative schools is often of limited value for education programming. Initial educational assessment is frequently cursory and incomplete for many students, often consisting of an initial screening to identify grade level scores in a few domains of academic achievement, through such measures as the Wide Range Achievement Test or the Test of Adult Basic Education. Specific assessment that might be used to select objectives rarely occurs within classrooms, and continuous assessment data generally are not formally collected relative to students' progression through the curriculum.

Few alternative schools have incorporated a systematic and consistently applied education-oriented evaluation system, and tools used for intake and screening are frequently out of date and very limited in scope (e.g., single-word recognition, no written expression, computation sample composed of only a few items). Furthermore, intake assessment results are seldom used for instruction planning, and teachers rarely use the scores to guide decision making about instruction.

Recommended Practices

Recognition and assessment of a student's needs — both for eligibility decision making and for the development of educational and treatment plans — is an essential function of most alternative programs. Functional assessment procedures should be tailored, therefore, to the purposes of evaluation, the needs of the student, and the curriculum of the school. Furthermore, assessment materials and procedures should be selected, administered, and interpreted in ways that allow adequate screening, the determination of program eligibility, and the development of a functional educational plan.

The evaluation procedures used when developing educational plans should not be limited to standardized tests but rather should include a careful analysis of the student's history, including interviews and reviews of classroom assignments. In addition, curriculum-based evaluation and measurement procedures should be employed, not only to select objectives, but also to monitor overall student performance and improvement. This point is stressed essentially because the testing used by teachers in alternative settings often is not aligned with the elements actually being taught.

To accomplish the just enumerated recommendations, academic and social skills curricula must be clarified and implemented. Functional assessment procedures can then be selected or developed to match this specified set of learning outcomes. Within many alternative programs, content as well as performance standards are left to the judgment of individual teachers. As a result, the quality of conclusions about student needs are often as diverse as staff opinion. In this sort of assessment context, many teachers come to view evaluation as an uninformative "hoop" to jump through. They also tend to plan instruction around activities and available materials because they do not have a clear sense of what individual students need to be taught.

Many teachers in alternative schools do an excellent job of selecting activities and delivering instruction. However, if the correct individual learning outcomes for individual students are not targeted (and their current levels of performance not accommodated to that outcome), progress will not result from even the best presentations.

Functional Curriculum

A functional curriculum is one that allows the program to meet a student's cognitive, vocational, social, and behavioral needs. Such a curriculum focuses on developing skills that are not only socially relevant but also job-related and geared to daily living. In addition to progressing through an academic curriculum, youth in alternative programs frequently need to begin by learning how to follow directions and progress toward learning how to find a job, live on a budget, use a telephone, purchase goods and services, interact appropriately with others, read a newspaper, use appropriate language, and run simple computer programs, not necessarily in that order.

Typical Practices in Many Alternative Programs

The goal of many alternative programs is simply to return students to the mainstream (Grosenick, George, & George, 1987), which usually entails teaching students the academic skills necessary to function in traditional educational settings. Because many students in alternative programs are not functioning at grade level in reading, mathematics, or other academic areas, serious questions can arise regarding whether an advanced, academically oriented curriculum covering traditional high school content has value for the majority of students in the program. When many students are reading significantly below grade level, attempts to complete high school credits or learn trigonometry may be irrelevant.

Recommended Practices

A common curriculum with a defined set of learner outcomes must be developed and adhered to by teachers. Ideally, such a curriculum is "packaged" into well-defined, cohesive, short units and accompanied by a placement test. Conversely, it may be foolish to undertake elaborate programs of study in many alternative programs simply because the flow of instruction is so often disrupted by newly arriving students as well as by students leaving without reaching a full understanding of the programs.

However, the cohesiveness of the program should not be short-changed. Many alternative schools adopt a short-unit format which in effect runs the student through units that are unconnected to previous learning experiences or personal needs. To avoid such an error and maintain a cohesive program, educators must be sure that units are clearly linked to one another. In addition, learning outcomes — if they are functional — should include standards. Content statements are not sufficient because teachers may hold disparate ideas about what constitutes a successful performance. They may also vary widely in their tolerance of inappropriate classroom behavior. This variance in expectations and tolerances underscores the need for assessment procedures that are aligned with the units of instruction and for setting passing scores on assessments that are understood and agreed upon by the staff.

In a fundamental way, the purpose of a functional curriculum is to emphasize daily living skills, as well as more traditional academic curriculum areas. Depending upon each student's educational strengths and weaknesses, emphasis upon obtaining Carnegie Units or moving from one grade level to another may not be realistic within the context of most alternative programs. Students with EBD, for example, frequently exhibit significant deficits in the domains of social skills, life skills, and vocational or career skills. Teaching these skills, therefore, should be a viable component of effective alternative school programs. Many commercially available social skills curricula have been used effectively in alternative programs and may well be worth considering.

Life skills training should focus on teaching students the daily living skills that lead to living independently in the larger community. They include teaching students the skills necessary to use a bus schedule, obtain a driver's license, obtain credit, use a newspaper to identify leisure activities or job opportunities, shop for food or other necessities, and live on a budget.

Finally, developing job, work, and career-related skills is critical for the eventual success of most alternative school students. While many alternative programs do not provide comprehensive vocational education programs on site, the development of basic work skills, coupled with job-related social and life skills, is a valuable component of an alternative curriculum. Opportunities for part-time employment and access to vocational training programs in the community are adjuncts to effective alternative programs.

Effective and Efficient Instruction

Teachers should be accountable for delivering instruction that specifically addresses short-term objectives and performance standards specified in a well-defined school-wide curriculum. Furthermore, teachers must systematically monitor student progress toward mastery of those objectives and standards, in the appropriate sequence and according to student needs. This may be accomplished by ensuring the alignment of instruction with plans based upon assessment instruments that are themselves aligned with the curriculum. This alignment requires a quality curriculum, appropriate assessment, and effective instruction. Therefore, the use of correct assessment procedures and a functional curriculum are not the only prerequisites for alignment. Instruction focusing on teaching to objectives is also needed.

Typical Practices in Many Alternative Programs

Instructional time is often not well used in many alternative schools. In fact, accumulated evidence suggests that the primary medium of instruction may be independent, non-interactive seatwork, often on identical tasks, supported by little, if any, direct instruction (CCBD & CASE, 1995). In some cases, students may receive help only when they ask for it. Such practices place the burden of error identification and monitoring on the students themselves. While this sort of self-monitoring is a prerequisite for self-control and, therefore, an *ideal* goal for education, it may be unrealistic to expect that students in alternative schools will automatically exercise this sort of judgment. If they could function that well, chances are they would not be in an alternative education placement.

Another major instructional problem apparent in many alternative classrooms is the large numbers of students frequently absent from class. Students are often truant from school or may be found in the school office, in the time-out area, or roaming the hallways. Even if they are in the classroom, many students are either off-task or disruptive.

Given this lack of structure in the classroom as well as the often ineffective and noninteractive instructional techniques used, there is little incentive for students to control their behavior. Because many students with EBD have been placed in alternative settings due to disruptive or antisocial behavior, classroom and school-wide behavior management systems are necessary but not always evident. Such is the continuing irony of alternative systems.

Recommended Practices

All teachers should be observed in their classrooms by supervisory staff to ensure that appropriate and effective educational services are delivered and to receive targeted consultative assistance regarding the delivery of that instruction, classroom behavior management, and educational decision making for individual students. If school staff lack the information needed to accomplish this sort of instruction and supervision, staff development activities must be available.

Transition

The effective transition of students (and their educational records) into and out of alternative programs is a critical component of any educationl plan. Hence, the focus of educational assessment, curricula, and instruction must be on providing students with the skills and knowledge to succeed in the community. This means the collaborative transition of students from alternative placements back into traditional educational settings must drive all aspects of alternative education (George, Valore, Quinn, & Varisco, in press). A clear example of applying a process approach to teaching the skills necessary to make successful transitions can be seen in the reintegration model used by the staff at the West Shore Day Treatment Center at Cleveland, Ohio's Positive Education Program. Their reintegration model is summarized in Appendix B.

Typical Practices in Many Alternative Programs

There is good reason to argue that the educational transition of students into many alternative schools is, at best, inadequate. While a good number of schools have developed intake procedures, few have initiated procedures for the successful transition of students who leave a program (Grosenick, George, George, & Lewis, 1991). For alternative schools serving students from a number of other schools or school districts, the transition of students into or out of alternative programs merely consists of the transfer of educational records, which is often piecemeal or late at best. Because of the relatively short stay of many students, it is sometimes difficult for even the records to catch up with the students.

Educational transition out of alternative education programs also is haphazard. Once a student leaves, education staff generally have no further information about what happens to a student, unless the student returns at a later time. There is no connection between the alternative education program and the public schools, group homes, community programs, or correctional programs to which students are sent. Educational records and information are often not transferred or are delayed to these programs, and alternative school staff get little outside feedback on the quality of their own work.

Once students are removed from traditional schools and placed in alternative school programs, there often is resistance, reluctance, and outright refusal to "bring them back" (Harrington-Lyeker, 1995). In addition, even if students were to return to public schools or other community settings with comprehensive and relevant educational information, there often is a serious lack of effective community transition and aftercare programs for these students. Many students, therefore, return to the alternative school; others end up in more restrictive placements.

Recommended Practices

The responsibility for student transition must be shared by the alternative education staff and by the public schools and other community-based or residential programs that send out and receive students. By providing comprehensive information concerning the abilities and strengths of their students, the alternative staff can make a major contribution to the process. One way to accomplish this for students with disabilities is to make transition plans and objectives clearly evident in every Individual Education Plan (IEP).

Comprehensive Systems

Comprehensive systems of appropriate educational services for students in alternative schools are provided so that all staff within the school and all agencies in the community can work in a coordinated manner to serve these students. Developing comprehensive systems means balancing often competing priorities of various agencies (e.g., social services, foster care agencies, child protective services, the juvenile justice system) and maintaining effective communication and cooperation among staff responsible for these youth. Unfortunately, experience tells us that it is extremely difficult to produce such a system when some students may be in an alternative program on a short-term basis, while others are there on a long-term basis.

Typical Practices in Many Alternative Programs

Comprehensive systems often do not exist in alternative programs — or prior to or following placement in such programs. The provision of effective educational services is, admittedly, difficult to achieve due to the sometimes conflicting priorities and responsibilities of alternative school staff and those within the social service, mental health, correctional, and educational agencies with whom many alternative school students come into contact.

Care and supervision define the function of alternative programs. However, the lack of comprehensive and coordinated administrative structures in many alternative schools frequently causes supervision and program functions to pose competing priorities. This may be because education, mental health, and social services do not appear to be closely linked to student needs. For example, there seems to be a number of "turf issues" that preclude effective programming for these youth, including students with disabilities, despite the required participation in their education of multidisciplinary teams.

The often limited team coordination and cooperation is apparent in the dearth of strong interagency linkages between education, social services, and mental health agencies in the community, and, as evidenced by the high number of youth who return to alternative programs, comprehensive linkages generally do not exist between the courts, the public schools, alternative schools, and aftercare programs. Aware of this, educators at an Alliance, Ohio, high school began a grassroots task force to confront these multiple problems. Appendix C summarizes the results of their efforts.

Recommended Practices

A system for providing "wraparound" services (Eber, 1977) can vastly improve efficiency especially when it is practiced in the form of appropriate individualized special education, and regular education, mental health, and social services. Coordinated, cooperative, and comprehensive services, both within the facility and within the community, must be designed to effectively serve students in alternative schools.

To be effective, a wraparound system must be a process for developing realistic behavior plans for students with EBD, which involve significant persons from all domains a the student's life. The focus of the plan must be on the strengths of the student and others in his or her life.

Availability of Appropriate Staff and Resources for Students with Disabilities

A significant proportion of students in most alternative education programs have disabilities. Accordingly, there is a growing sentiment that staff need to be composed of certified special education teachers and support staff who have extensive training in how to serve students with disabilities. In addition, alternative programs must focus on providing a full continuum of educational services and due process protections for students with disabilities and their families. Appendix D presents an overview of the certification issue in California.

Typical Practices in Many Alternative Programs

If it can be assumed that special education procedural requirements are in the student's best interest, then it can be argued that the promise of the special education mandate is not being met in many alternative programs. In fact, in some so-called "charter" schools, because there are no certified teachers, parents are required to withdraw their children from special education eligibility in order to be placed in such an alternative program. This is all the more disturbing given the general recognition that the population not being served is in great need of special education services and due process protections.

In addition to the shortage of certified special education teachers in many alternative schools, a continuum of educational services does not seem to be in place for students with disabilities. And, unless the alternative program is specifically designed to meet the individual needs of students with disabilities, a range of placement options is generally not available.

Recommended Practices

Multidisciplinary treatment programs must be established in alternative education programs. This means that the program must provide a full complement of appropriately certified special education teachers, as well as provide access to related-services personnel. (In addition, the school should provide extensive and comprehensive inservice training for education and other program staff.) Inservice training should focus on developing and providing functional assessment procedures, functional curricula, effective and efficient instructional techniques, and educational transition services to develop systems of care within the alternative school and for students returning to the public schools or to the community. Inservice training also should focus on procedures for supporting and improving compre-

hensive wraparound services in the form of multidisciplinary inter-
actions and decision making. Without this effort to provide consider-
able resources, alternative school staff will not come together to serve
students.

Conclusion 6

The basic philosophy of special education is that the traditional "one-size-fits-all" approach to educating students is not universally effective. Stated positively, as long as the needs of students vary, programs must be designed to address those special needs and to educate children (despite their problems) in a variety of ways. This philosophy is perhaps no more clearly demonstrated than in the case of children and youth with emotional, behavioral, or social disorders, whose very behavior threatens their success in traditional education settings.

The special mission of alternative placements, although varying in degree from program to program, is to meet the individual needs of students served. Within that philosophical context, some programs see their role as strictly punitive in nature, while others see themselves as providers of "treatment" designed to reintegrate their students into the educational mainstream.

Regardless of philosophy, programs that include components of functional analysis, functional assessment, effective teaching, transition planning, comprehensive systems, and specialized teacher training and resources are more effective at successfully meeting the special needs of the children and youth in their care than are those programs generally seen as "reactionary" in their approach.

We suspect that there are more programs in need of reform than there are exemplary programs. Therefore, all professionals who care about the needs of children and youth with emotional, behavioral, and social disorders have a long way to go toward ensuring that every child in America reaches her or his educational as well as "real-life" potential. It is only through beneficial changes in programs, and through sound research and practice, that such a distance can, in fact, be covered.

References

7

American Federation of Teachers. (1993). *Draft AFT position on inclusion.* (Available from American Federation of Teachers, 555 New Jersey Ave., N.W., Washington, D.C., 20001).

Ashcroft, R. (1987). A conceptual model for assessing levels of interpersonal skill. *Teaching: Behaviorally Disordered Youth, 3,* 10-21.

Ashcroft, R., Price, T., & McNair, J. (1992). Teacher perceived training needs in institutional and alternative settings. *Journal for Juvenile Justice and Detention Services, 7*(1), 41-47.

Ball, A. (1997). The Dallas County Juvenile Justice Alternative Education System. *Reaching Today's Youth, 1*(2), 63-64.

Council for Children with Behavioral Disorders & Council of Administrators of Special Education. (1995). *A joint statement on violence in the schools.* Reston, VA: Author. (ERIC Document Reproduction Service No. ED3868678)

Council for Exceptional Children. (1993). *CEC policy on inclusive schools and community settings.* Reston, VA: The Council for Exceptional Children.

Council of Administrators of Special Education. (1994). *CASE position paper on delivery of services to students with disabilities.* (Available from Council for Exceptional Children, 1920 Association Drive, Reston, VA 20191-1589).

Eber, L. (1997). Improving school-based behavioral interventions through use of the wraparound process. *Reaching Today's Youth, 1*(2), 32-36.

Egnor, D. (1996). IDEA reauthorization and the debate on schools' disciplinary procedures under IDEA. *Focus on Exceptional Children, 29*(4), 17-22.

Fizzell, R., & Raywid, M. A. (1997). If alternative schools are the answer ... what's the question? *Reaching Today's Youth, 1*(2), 7-9.

Fuller, C. G., & Sabatino, D. A. (1996). Who attends alternative high schools? *The High School Journal, 79,* 292-297.

George, M. P., Valore, T., Quinn, M. M., & Varisco, R. (in press). Preparing to go home: A collaborative approach to transition. *Preventing School Failure.*

Glass, R. S. (1994). Alternative schools. *American Teacher, 79,* 10-11, 18.

Grosenick, J. K., George, M. P., & George, N. L. (1987). A profile of school programs for the behaviorally disordered: Twenty years after Morse, Cutler, and Fink. *Behavioral Disorders, 12,* 159-168.

Grosenick, J. K., George, N. L., George, M. P., & Lewis, T. J. (1991). Public school services for behaviorally disordered students: Program practices in the 1980s. *Behavioral Disorders, 16,* 87-96.

Harrington-Lueker, D. (1995). Ideas for alternative schools for troubled kids. *American School Board Journal, 181,* 16-21.

Hobbs, N. (1975). *The futures of children.* San Francisco: Jossey-Bass.

Honig v. Doe, 484 U.S. 305,323 (1988).

Howell, K. W., Fox, S., & Morehead, M. K. (1993). *Curriculum-based evaluation: Teaching and decision-making.* Belmont, CA: Wadsworth.

Individuals with Disabilities Act Amendments of 1997. Pub.L.No. 105-17 (1997).

Leone, P. E., Rutherford, R. B., & Nelson, C. M. (1991). *Special education in juvenile correntions.* Reston, VA: Council for Exceptional Children.

MacMillan, D. L., Gresham, F. M., & Forness, S. R. (1996). Full inclusion: An empirical perspective. *Behavioral Disorders, 21,* 145-159.

National Association of State Boards of Education. (1992). *Winners all: From mainstreaming to inclusion.* (Available from National Association of State Boards of Education, 1012 Cameron Street, Alexandria, VA 22314).

Raywid, M. A. (1994). Alternative schools: The state of the art. *Educational Leadership, 52*(1), 26-31.

Rutherford, R. B., & Howell, K. W. (1997). Education program assessment: MacLaren Children's Center School. Los Angeles: Los Angeles County Department of Child and Family Services.

Rutherford, R. B., Nelson, C. M., & Wolford, B. I. (1985). Special education in the most restrictive environment: Correctional/special education. *Journal of Special Education, 19*(1), 59-71.

Smink, J. (1997). All students can learn: Best practices for alternative schooling. *Reaching Today's Youth, 1*(2), 65-68.

Appendices

Appendix A
The Compass Center:
An Effective Alternative

The Compass Center is a collaborative, nontraditional campus composed of three programs serving at-risk children and youth. Referral to any of the Compass Center programs is initiated on the home-school campus. Each campus benefits from the presence of an on-site teacher-assistance team composed of mentor teachers. All requests for prereferral assistance are routed through this support system, through which appropriate interventions are suggested and evaluated. If warranted, the teacher-assistance team or home-campus principal make a referral to the district placement committee, who examines the interventions attempted and makes recommendations for continued campus intervention or placement in one of the Compass Center programs.

Texas law makes removal from peers mandatory for such offenses as (a) engaging in conduct punishable as a felony; (b) assault; (c) possession, selling, or under the influence of a controlled substance; (d) engaging in public lewdness; (e) possession of a firearm or illegal knife; and (f) indecency with a child (Texas Senate Bill 1, Chapter 37, Sections 37.006 and 37.007, 1995). Following the District Placement Committee's recommendations and other due process dialogues and procedures deemed necessary, a student may be placed in DIRECT (Direct Individual Responsibility through Education, Correction, and Training) for these offenses. Striving to meet the educational needs of students in Grades 4 through 12 who have traditionally been expelled from school, DIRECT provides a setting wherein ecological assessment and provision of services are emphasized.

Initially, through interviews, behavioral rating scales, and a review of behavioral data accumulated by the student's home school, information is triangulated and target behaviors are identified. Following this formative assessment, certified Compass Center personnel, as well as staff from other community mental health/mental retardation clinics, the Anderson Cherokee Community Enrichment ServiceS (ACCESS), and/or county juvenile probation officers, evaluate the target behaviors and initiate observations within the classroom setting. Subsequent to these reviews, the Compass Center in-school psychology specialist and the director analyze the appropriateness of identified target behaviors, and intervention priorities are established. Additionally, academic or psychological deficits are identified for further testing.

Focus is then directed toward prioritized target behaviors in either an individual or group format, with all interventions directly tied to individual needs. Nevertheless, interventions may include group social skills training, aggression replacement training, and instruction in relaxation techniques.

Overwhelmingly, the bearing in DIRECT is toward individual responsibility. Within such a framework, prominence is given to an individual's "bonding" with the community, and, in order to exit the program, students must demonstrate mastery and community generalization of target behaviors.

Leslie Brinkman George
Director
Compass Center
Jacksonville Independent School District
Jacksonville, Texas

Appendix B
The Positive Education Program: Reintegration Model

At West Shores, teachers begin with the end in sight. As soon as a student enters the alternative day-treatment program for students with severe emotional and behavioral problems, preparation for reintegration into their home schools begins. Through classroom observations and meetings with home-school personnel, the case manager identifies key features of the new setting, such as information on instructional methods and academic demands of the receiving teachers, how student performance is assessed, how feedback is delivered, which curriculum materials are used, and the rules and procedures unique to the setting. The case manager may even collect copies of books and materials that the student will eventually use from the receiving school. All of this information is shared with the student, parents, and the teachers at the treatment center and is incorporated into his or her daily routine.

Realizing that successful reintegration depends upon the collaborative effort of the referring school, the family, the alternative day treatment program, and any other agency involved with the student, collectively form the student's treatment team. This team, in conjunction with the student, develops a plan to ensure that the student acquires all of the skills necessary for successful reintegration.

While at West Shore, students learn skills beyond those usually offered by most traditional educational systems. Basically, students learn skills to replace negative, inappropriate, or maladaptive behaviors with appropriate home, school, and community behavior. While the student is learning these skills, the rules of the home school are in effect within the treatment center. In addition, the student receives only those types of privileges available in the home school.

When a student feels he or she has acquired the skills required by the home school, he or she declares a readiness with a "petition for graduation," within which the student describes in his or her own words the behaviors that initially led to referral, how he or she has improved, and how potential problematic situations will be handled in the home school setting. After the student completes the petition, it is routed to all involved staff.

The petition is then either accepted or changes are discussed. Eventually, because it serves many purposes, the petition is signed by all staff and the student. First, it stresses the link between the student's inappropriate behaviors and the consequences of those behaviors (placement in the alternative day treatment setting). Next, the important connection is made between the appropriate behaviors learned at the treatment center and the consequences of those behaviors (returning to school). This process generates a feeling of accomplishment and helps by providing the student with some status. This is important, as an abundance of privileges is no longer available to the student.

Following the petition, the case manager from the treatment center continues the liaison work between the home school, treatment center, home, and other involved agencies. It is the case manager's responsibility to establish a support system for the reintegrating student. In the home-school setting, a building advocate is identified. This person could be anyone — teacher, aide, lunchroom assistant, custodian, coach, counselor, or the like with whom the student is comfortable. The building advocate, who is accessible and willing to become familiar with the returning student's strengths and weaknesses, helps monitor the student's progress, ensures that academic and behavior plans are followed, helps problem-solve crisis situations, and celebrates the student's successes. The building advocate becomes an integral part of the communication system between the home school and treatment center.

Before the actual transition, the student and case manager arrange to visit the home-school setting. During this visit, the student is allowed to make a detailed examination of every setting that he or she may encounter after reintegration (the transportation area, classroom(s), cafeteria, restrooms, the nurse's office, and any other area that may be important). The student usually has an opportunity to observe the classroom(s) that he or she will attend and to discuss with the teacher, among other things, classroom rules and expectations. Sometimes students even have a chance to introduce themselves to and mingle with future classmates. A critical part of the home-school visit is time spent developing a positive relationship with the principal of the school and the student's building advocate.

For some students, reintegration and even the home-school visit can be very difficult. Because the alternative placement is often a safe, predictable, and secure environment where they have been successful (perhaps for the first time in their academic lives), some students begin to sabotage their reintegration by displaying some of the inappropriate behaviors that led to their alternative-setting placement in the first place. It is important to look beyond their inappropriate behavior and take steps to ease their anxiety. A gradual desensitization process often helps to reduce angst during this time. In sensitive cases such as these, the process can begin with the reintegrating student's teacher (or other staff member who has a close and trusting relationship) starting the visitation process by driving to the school but remaining in the car. Student and teacher would then return to the treatment center and talk about the experience and prepare for the next step. Subsequent visits may include driving into the school's parking lot, getting out of the car and walking around the exterior of the building, and entering the school and walking through the hallways. All of this might need to be repeated several times prior to the visitation that includes meeting school personnel and visiting the classrooms.

Once the decision has been made to reintegrate the student on a full-time basis, the student is considered a graduate of the alternative treatment center, and the staff and classmates plan a celebration. During the graduation ceremony, all visitors (family, friends, home-school personnel) are introduced to each other and the reintegrating student receives a diploma to signify his or her achievement and completion of the alternative school's treatment program. Personal congratulations, speeches, cards, and gifts are exchanged. This graduation ceremony is the culminating activity that allows the student and his or her parents to feel a sense of accomplishment and pride for all of the challenges faced and hard work endured. The graduation ceremony also provides a similar feeling for staff and produces a sense of hope for students at the center still working toward graduation.

Attention to detail, beginning with the end in sight and working collaboratively with all of the individuals significant to this process, has increased the success rate of students reintegrating from PEP to their home schools. In fact, data demonstrate that approximately 85% of students are successful in their home school during their first year. Compared to the national average of 20% (Grosenick, George, George, & Lewis, 1991), perhaps other alternative programs should take notice.

Thomas Valore
Program Coordinator
West Shore Day Treatment Center
Cleveland, Ohio

Appendix C
Alliance Family Council:
A Comprehensive Approach
to Systematic Change

The mission of the Alliance Family Council in Alliance, Ohio, is to facilitate collaboration and cooperation to develop a system that empowers families and community institutions to work together to reduce the problems that plague the juveniles of Alliance. Specifically, the youth-oriented goals include the reduction of inappropriate classroom and community behavior and an increase in readiness to learn and academic achievement.

The idea for a collaborative task force of this nature came about when school officials noticed a rise in violent behavior of students, followed by increased suspensions and expulsions. Examination of this problem revealed that many of the students who were in trouble in school were also having problems in the community. In response to this dilemma, a small group of people representing the school district and juvenile courts and probation joined together to confront the problem and search for solutions. What they found was that each agency had the same goal — to help juveniles who were having problems and their families — and faced similar budget and staffing constraints. They soon realized also that much of their individual efforts were simply duplicating those of other agencies. Working together with other agencies, such as the Department of Human Services and Child and Adolescent Mental Health, this group decided to change the system in order to be more effective and efficient.

The task force improved service delivery by appointing a case manager to families who needed services. The case manger was responsible to work collaboratively with agencies in creating a coordinated service plan to ensure that families received all of the services they needed while streamlining the process by requiring only one set of entry paperwork rather than duplicating the effort at each individual agency.

To help the professionals in each agency work together, individuals participated in cross-training. Whenever one agency held training sessions, individuals from other agencies were invited to participate. This allowed insight into what each agency did and input from others.

Before the Council began their efforts to improve services for the families in Alliance City, many families who needed mental health services did not receive them. Many families found it difficult to simply get to the mental health agencies, due both to the physical location and to the stigma of being seen walking into such an agency. To address this issue, the mental health agency rented space from the school and set up shop in local schools. This provided easy and less stigmatizing access for families, as well as support to teachers who were having difficulties with their students.

Agencies began collaborating in many different ways. They collaborated in grant writing efforts and were awarded many small grants to make more community improvements for juveniles and families. They became more committed to supporting one another in more concrete ways. For example, representatives from the schools actually attended juvenile court hearings rather than just calling or faxing requested information. Hearing officers soon found that the educators had valuable insights into problems and offered suggestions for interventions and accommodations that could be accomplished at school. Because of their proximity, mental health counselors were able to attend expulsion and suspension hearings at the schools. Many times the problems that precipitated the expulsion or suspension were more deeply rooted than merely problems in school. For instance, many students with school problems also had problems with alcohol (either themselves directly or their families). Because mental health counselors were present, those issues could be addressed — and parents were more receptive to both the decision of the school and the offer of help.

As a result of the efforts of the Council, the waiting list for services has decreased dramatically, more families are taking advantage of mental health counseling, and parent volunteerism has increased in the schools. Discipline problems in the schools and community also have decreased, and students are making improvements in their academic studies as well. Because of the comprehensive system of services, students can concentrate on the challenge of learning, rather than on the many other problems facing today's children and youth.

Theresa Lattanzi
Director (Emeritus)
Alliance Family and Children First Council
Alliance City Schools, Ohio

Appendix D
Availability of Appropriate Staff and Resources for Students in Alternative Settings: Emerging Themes and Recommendations

Young people who become involved with law enforcement may continue their education in one or more of a wide array of settings. To illustrate this point, provisions available in the State of California will be presented.

In California, students who have been adjudicated by the juvenile courts or are at risk of adjudication frequently are assigned to non-traditional, alternative educational settings such as

1. Home teaching or independent study.

2. Classes organized primarily for adults.

3. Hospital classes.

4. Necessary small high schools.

5. Continuation schools.

6. Alternative schools.

7. Juvenile court schools.

8. County community schools.

These programs are authorized in Section 44865 & 44867 of the California Education Code which further stipulates that teachers who serve in these settings should hold a regular teaching credential and a "special fitness to perform." No other reference to qualifications is given and no special training is required for teachers.

In California, the number of at-risk youth taught in alternative settings rivals the total number of students served in special education (Ashcroft, 1987). In contrast to special education, a field of study that has generated in California alone six different specialist teacher credentials, few universities offer a single course for teachers of adjudicated and at-risk youth. Teachers who work with youth in alternative settings typically receive no specialized training intended to equip them to serve these often difficult-to-teach students in the context of these atypical instructional settings. In addition, when students with Individual Education Plans (IEPs) are referred to alternative placements, they are often exited from special education, making the alternative education teacher's role even more complex.

Teachers in alternative instructional settings perceive that their pre-service training is not adequate. When alternative education teachers were surveyed (Ashcroft, Price, & McNair, 1992) about the efficacy of their alternative education training, most had received no specialized training. A few identified inservice workshops and self-education as the source and extent of their training.

Although preparation for academic instruction was frequently identified as adequate, many alternative education teachers were assigned to teaching subject matter outside their specialty. One likely reason is that a common instructional setting in alternative education is the self-contained classroom, requiring a teacher to be well-versed in many subject areas. The specific nonacademic areas that teachers felt the least prepared to address were the social, emotional, psychological, behavioral, special learning, and legal problems faced by their students. Teachers overwhelmingly indicated they would participate in appropriate training if it were available.

Three themes emerge:

1. Students placed in institutional and alternative instructional settings are perceived by their teachers as presenting atypical learning needs.

2. Teachers in these settings perceive themselves as inadequately prepared to address these atypical needs.

3. Teachers want appropriate training.

From the emerging themes, three recommendations can be made to improve availability of appropriate staff and resources for students with disabilities. In the first place, the competencies for teaching in alternative settings must be identified. Second, preservice training programs should address the need for specific training for instruction in alternative settings. Finally, teaching in alternative settings should be recognized as a legitimate career path for educators with its own training paradigm and licensure.

Richard Ashcroft
Associate Professor
California State University, San Bernadino